FRESH-CUT
Flowers
FOR A
FRIEND

Dianna
BOOHER

J COUNTRYMAN®

www.jcountryman.com
A division of Thomas Nelson, Inc.
www.thomasnelson.com

Copyright © 2002 by Dianna Booher.

Published by J. Countryman, a division of Thomas Nelson, Inc., Nashville, Tennessee, 37214.

Edited by Terri Gibbs

Published in association with the literary agency of Alive Communications, 1465 Kelly Johnson Blvd., Suite 320, Colorado Springs, CO 80920

Designed by Garborg Design Works, Minneapolis, Minnesota

Photos by Lisa Garborg

www.thomasnelson.com

ISBN: 0-8499-9610-4

Printed and bound in USA.

You may not be in a class
by yourself, but it sure doesn't
take long to call the roll.

BUM PHILLIPS

Your friendship is special to me.
Of acquaintances, there are many.
Of casual friends, there are many.
But close friends—they are few.

When I think about the times we've spent together, the best memories are those when we did nothing special. We simply talked, walked, lived.

A friend is someone
you can do
nothing with,
and enjoy it.

ANONYMOUS

We can do not great things;

only small things

with great love.

MOTHER TERESA

*In thinking about our friendship,
it's not the big things that stand out.
It's the many, many small things
that show how much you care.*

Friendship is
unnecessary,
like philosophy,
like art....
It has no survival
value; rather it is one
of those things that
give value to survival.

C. S. LEWIS

I could live without friends.
But what a depressing thought!
A friendship like ours gives definition
to that old phrase "the good life."

I have counted on you like family. Thanks for taking their place in so many times of need.

Do not forsake your own friend or your father's friend, nor go to your brother's house in the day of your calamity; better is a neighbor nearby than a brother far away.

PROVERBS 27:10

A conversation here.
A conversation there.
A meal. A trip. A visit.
A problem faced.
A struggle overcome.
A success shared. Little by little,
our friendship has grown.

True friendship

is a plant

of slow growth.

GEORGE
WASHINGTON

The world is so empty if
one thinks only of mountains,
rivers, and cities; but to know
someone here and there who
thinks and feels with us, and
who, though distant, is close
to us in spirit, this makes the
earth an inhabited garden.

GÓETHE

Friends don't have to say hello or
good-bye. Like a neighbor who
pops in to borrow a cup of sugar,
you can pop back into my life in a
day or a year and it's as though
we've never missed a beat.

Be very careful in the
selection of your friends:
"the most valuable and
fairest furniture of life."

CICERO

Some people are always
glad to shake my hand when
I'm in the limelight. Fewer want
to join me when I've committed
a colossal goof. But you?
You've been there when I've
succeeded or when I've failed.

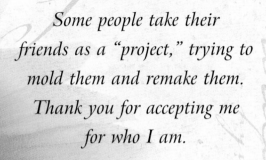

*Some people take their
friends as a "project," trying to
mold them and remake them.
Thank you for accepting me
for who I am.*

Love is blind;
friendship
closes its eyes.

ANONYMOUS

Thank you for stretching me.
For helping me to see
new ways of relating,
new causes to consider,
new interests to explore.

Friendship is a horizon—
which expands whenever
we approach it.

E. R. HAZLIP

Friendship multiplies
the good of life and
divides the evil.

BALTASAR GRACIAN

Sharing the happy-nings
in my life with you
has doubled my pleasure.
The same is true for the
disappointments—you've
made the doldrums
more bearable.

We don't choose our families, but friends are up for grabs. I'm glad to choose you. You are as close as family—if not closer.

Friends are relatives you make for yourself.

EUSTACHE DESCHAMPS

Silences make the real
conversations between friends.
Not the saying but the never
needing to say is what counts.

MARGARET RUNBECK

Silences are never awkward
with you. We share quiet
companionship without
having to make excuses.
I'm comfortable with that.

I don't think it was luck
that our paths crossed.
Your friendship is one
of God's gifts designed
especially for me.

You don't just luck into
things as much as you'd
like to think you do. You build
step by step, whether it's
friendships or opportunities.

BARBARA BUSH

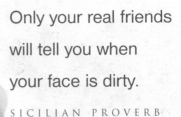

Only your real friends
will tell you when
your face is dirty.

SICILIAN PROVERB

Thank you for saying
things to me that have
not always been easy to say.
You risk my hurt, disappointment,
and anger. But you say them
anyway. I appreciate that.

The most important thing we share is our faith. When either of us feels totally alone, let's pledge to remind each other of God's love.

There is a friend
who sticks closer
than a brother.

PROVERBS 18:24

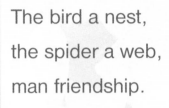

The bird a nest,

the spider a web,

man friendship.

WILLIAM BLAKE

You are my hearth on
cold winter days.

At times, I've taken great liberty in telling you what I think. Maybe I've said what you didn't really want to hear. But thank you for listening anyway.

Better to be a nettle
in the side of your
friend than his echo.

RALPH WALDO EMERSON

Thank you being loyal to me, for holding my secrets safe. I trust you implicitly.

There can be no friendship without confidence, and no confidence without integrity.

SAMUEL JOHNSON

We should get into
the habit of reading
inspirational books,
looking at inspirational
pictures, hearing
inspirational music,
associating with
inspirational friends.

ALFRED A.
MONTAPERT

Like great music, art,
literature, and nature . . .
you inspire me.

When a friend is in trouble,
don't annoy him by asking
if there is anything you
can do. Think up something
appropriate and do it.

EDGAR WATSON HOWE

Without my ever having
to ask, you always seem
to know just what to do.
That makes it doubly nice—what
you've done and what
I didn't have to ask.

You read between
the lines when I'm not
being transparent.
You push me beyond the
borders of mediocrity.

As iron sharpens iron,
so a man sharpens the
countenance of his friend.

PROVERBS 27:17

I value the friend

who for me finds time

on his calendar, but

I cherish the friend

who for me does not

consult the calendar.

ROBERT BRAULT

Thanks for always
making my calls
and visits welcome.

I like the little rituals
and inside jokes we share.
They weave our past
together tightly and
promise joys for tomorrow.

Wishing to
be friends is
quick work,
but friendship is
slow-ripening fruit.

ARISTOTLE

When we are young,
friends are, like everything
else, a matter of course.
In the old days we know
what it means to have them.

EDWARD GRIEG

When I was growing up a friend
was someone to talk with at
recess and do things with on the
weekends. But as I've gotten older,
friends have come to mean
so much more. They are not
pastimes—they are the main events.

The proper office of a friend
is to side with you when
you are in the wrong.
Nearly anybody will side with
you when you are right.

MARK TWAIN

*Thanks for speaking up for
me and for taking my side—
even when it is not the
popular thing to do. Loyalty
rates high in my book.*

You are not always
easy on me. And that's
exactly what I need.
Sometimes I feel
that you are the voice
of God in my life.

Faithful are the
wounds of a friend,
but the kisses of an
enemy are deceitful.

PROVERBS 27:6

I'm glad I don't have to censor my thoughts with you. Certainly everything that runs through my mind shouldn't come out my mouth—but with you, I'm safe. You're a great sounding board.

A friend is a person with whom I may be sincere. Before him I may think aloud.

RALPH WALDO EMERSON

In every friend we
lose a part of ourselves,
and the best part.

ALEXANDER POPE

I hope that through our friendship
I've enriched your life in some
small way. You have certainly
made me richer by far. You've
soaked up my heart and
"translated" me to the world.

A friend is one who
takes me for what I am.

HENRY DAVID THOREAU

*We've gone through
emotional highs and
emotional lows.
Our friendship is not
threatened by either—
it grows with both.*

You make me laugh—
even when life is
far from funny.

A merry heart
does good,
like a medicine.

PROVERBS 17:22

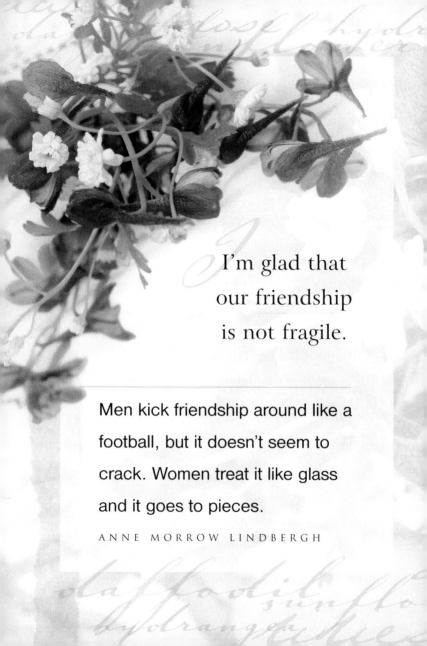

I'm glad that
our friendship
is not fragile.

Men kick friendship around like a
football, but it doesn't seem to
crack. Women treat it like glass
and it goes to pieces.

ANNE MORROW LINDBERGH

STAY is a

charming word in a

friend's vocabulary.

AMOS BRONSON
ALCOTT

Too many times, with some
of my ongoing conflicts
and issues, you've stayed until
the wee hours to hear me out,
and it's in those times that
you've meant the most.

We challenge
each other
to be funnier
and smarter.

ANNIE GOTTLIEB

Thanks for all the great
laughter we've shared.
You have a wonderful
sense of always seeing
the lighter side of life.

True friendship
is not measured
in days or decades.

Depth of
friendship
does not
depend upon
length of
acquaintance.

RABINDRANATH
TAGORE

Two are better than one,
because they have a
good reward for their labor.
For if they fall, one will lift
up his companion. But woe
to him who is alone when
he falls, for he has no one
to help him up.

ECCLESIASTES 4:9-10

In so many situations, you have
been the difference between
failure and success for me.
Thank you for being my backup.
We make a great team!

A friend is a present
you give yourself.

ROBERT LOUIS
STEVENSON

Every time we get
together, it feels like
Christmas morning!

I'm proud to have you
call me "friend"—it's a badge
I wear with honor.

A mirror reflects
a man's face, but
what he is really like
is shown by the kind
of friends he chooses.

PROVERBS 27:19 TLB

*There doesn't seem to be an
envious bone in your body!
Thanks for being successful and
happy enough in your own right
that you can enjoy the good
things that come my way.*

If there is any
sin more deadly
than envy, it is
being pleased at
being envied.

RICHARD ARMOUR

He who covers a transgression
seeks love, but he who repeats
a matter separates friends.

PROVERBS 17:9

You don't simmer with sympathy
over my weaknesses; you
summon my strengths. I'm a
better person because of you.

A mere friend
will agree with
you, but a real
friend will argue.

RUSSIAN PROVERB

With some friends, I talk work.
With some, I talk family.
With some, I talk pastimes.
But with you, there's no
subject too big or too small.

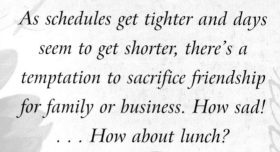

As schedules get tighter and days seem to get shorter, there's a temptation to sacrifice friendship for family or business. How sad! . . . How about lunch?

A friend is one who takes you to lunch even though you are not tax deductible.

ANONYMOUS

Thanks for encouraging me when I don't have confidence in myself. Those little pushes from you pay big dividends.

Indeed, we do not really live unless we have friends surrounding us like a firm wall against the winds of the world.

CHARLES HANSON TOWNE

My friends are my estate.
Forgive me then the
avarice to hoard them!

EMILY DICKINSON

Hours spent with you
are some of the happiest—
and most insightful.

How wonderful to have a wise friend like you. When I can't see the forest for the trees, you pull back the leaves and say, "Look again."

The pleasantness of one's friend springs from his earnest counsel.

PROVERBS 27:9

A faithful friend is
an image of God.

FRENCH PROVERB

Someone has said that God has
no hands but ours . . . no feet
but ours. Sometimes you are
God's hands and feet in my life.

Friendship lies on
a long continuum
of intensity.

THOMAS MOORE

Our friendship ebbs and flows
in its intensity. When I have a
problem that pulls me ashore
like the tide, you move toward
me like a swift current to offer
concern. When I'm feeling free
and independent, you let me
ride the waves alone.

Friendship based
solely upon gratitude
is like a photograph;
with time it fades.

CARMEN SYLVA

Our friendship rests
on the best, not the worst,
in both of us. We both
bring to the table wisdom—
only on different topics.

When I listen to the news,
watch television, or read
the paper, it seems the
whole world runs on gossip.
Thank you for always
believing the best about me
and not letting someone's
idle words ruin my reputation
or our relationship.

A gossip separates
close friends.

PROVERBS 16:28

You understand the contradictions in me that sometimes cause others to misunderstand me. With you, I can breathe more freely.

We are all travelers in the wilderness of this world, and the best that we find in our travels is an honest friend.

ROBERT LOUIS
STEVENSON

A true friend is

somebody who can

make us do what we can.

RALPH WALDO EMERSON

I'm often tempted to give up on
myself or my dream too soon.
Thank you for encouraging
me to reach for the stars.

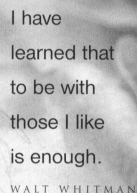

I have
learned that
to be with
those I like
is enough.

WALT WHITMAN

Leisure time is too precious these days
to waste with those whose company we
don't enjoy. In case I haven't said so,
I enjoy spending time with you.

Never injure
a friend,
even in jest.

CICERO

*You have never hurt me by
what you've said or done.
And that's a claim few
can make—even family.*

Our friendship has not been by chance. God sent you into my life for a special purpose. Thanks for being His friend to me.

Before you can help make the world right, you must be made right within.

JOHN MILLER

The refining pot is for silver
and the furnace for gold,
and a man is valued by what
others say of him.

PROVERBS 27:21

*I appreciate all the uplifting
things you say about me
and my efforts. But as my
friend, please don't ever let
me become full of myself.*

The better part
of one's life consists
of his friendships.

ABRAHAM LINCOLN

When I consider my past—all
my memories as a child, as a
youth, and as an adult—the
most vivid memories are not
of events but of friends. I've
come to mark and measure
my life by the friends I've
been privileged to know.

I treasure our talks.
That emotional connection
is vital to my well-being.

Friendship is the inexpressible

comfort of feeling safe with a

person, having neither to weigh

thoughts nor measure words.

GEORGE ELLIOT

The real secret
of happiness is
not what you
give or what you
receive; it's what
you share.

ANONYMOUS

I'm so grateful that you share
your life with me—the small
events, the casual thoughts,
the deepest heartaches.

I've done and said some crazy things in your presence. It feels so comfortable not to have to worry about how I'm coming across with you. I can try out new ideas for your honest reaction.

It is one of the blessings of old friends that you can afford to be stupid with them.

RALPH WALDO EMERSON

When I tell you of the happiness in my life, one look at your face tells me there's not an ounce of envy in you. Thanks for being such a true friend.

A heart at peace gives life to the body, but envy rots the bones.

PROVERBS
14:30 NIV

Friendship
demands attention.

THOMAS MOORE

You show courtesy . . .
you do not impose . . .
you ask first . . .
you listen quietly . . .
you stay late . . .
you arrive early . . .
you help without being asked . . .
you make time.

How long has it been since we've spent an entire day together? Much too long. You have a way of renewing my energy and enthusiasm for life.

Some of the most rewarding and beautiful moments of a friendship happen in the unforeseen open spaces between planned activities. It is important that you allow these spaces to exist.

CHRISTINE
LEEFELDT

Thank you for letting
me give to you in small
ways and in big ways.
All of us grow by giving.

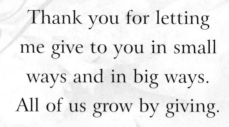

It takes great
generosity
to accept
generosity.

MERLE SHAIN

All that is not eternal
is out of date.

C.S. LEWIS

I admire your attention
to the important rather
than the trivial. Your life is
constantly lived to lay up
treasures in heaven.

Friendship is one of the sweetest joys of life. Many might have failed beneath the bitterness of their trial had they not found a friend.

CHARLES SPURGEON

Friendship satisfies a longing that no other relationship can match. I feel disconnected when I am separated from close friends like you.

I don't want to take you for granted. Please know how much I appreciate our friendship. I'll cherish our easy relationship always.

True

friendship is

like sound health, the value of

it is seldom known until it is lost.

C.C. COLTON

*Thanks for being my eyes
and ears on the world. I benefit
from your interactions with
others. Your network eventually
becomes my network;
your perspective, my perspective.*

Friends are like windows

through which you see

out into the world and

back into yourself. . . .

If you don't have friends

you see much less than

you otherwise might.

MERLE SHAIN

Dear
Friend...
♡

Friendship is like money,
easier made than kept.

SAMUEL BUTLER

Can you believe we've been
friends for so long? As with
any other great achievement,
I feel like celebrating!

A friend loves
at all times, and
a brother is born
for adversity.

PROVERBS 17:17

Maybe the one good
thing in a difficult day
is finding out how much
we need our friends.

*Our friendship provides me
with plenty of choices. You
never make me feel guilty
when I have to say no.*

Friendship is a
sheltering tree.

SAMUEL TAYLOR
COLERIDGE

He who throws away a
friend is as bad as he
who throws away his life.

SOPHOCLES

Someone has said that
sooner or later we
outgrow our friends.
I disagree. Though the
stages of friendships
change, our friendship
will last a lifetime.

There is no friend like an old friend

Who has shared our morning days,

No greeting like his welcome,

No homage like his praise.

OLIVER WENDELL HOLMES

Thank you for always taking
the time to offer compliments.
Words of praise coming from
you mean a lot because I
value your opinion so deeply.

You have certainly seen and
heard the worst in me—and yet,
you still call me your friend.

A blessed thing it is for
any man or woman to
have a friend, one human
soul whom we can trust
utterly, who knows the
best and worst of us,
and who loves us in
spite of all our faults.

CHARLES KINGSLEY

Don't you wish you had a dollar for each minute you've listened to me grumble about this or that? Rest assured that your listening has not been wasted. My telling you kept me from telling the rest of the world!

To hear complaints with patience, even when complaints are vain, is one of the duties of friendship.

SAMUEL JOHNSON

One of the most
beautiful qualities
of true friendship is
to understand and
to be understood.

SENECA

Raising our children. Dealing with our parents. Relating to our spouses. Detail upon detail. Conversation after conversation. Event after event. With one experience piling upon another, I've concluded that for each other we are one of life's necessities.

The only way
to have a friend
is to be one.

RALPH WALDO
EMERSON

Thank you for all the lovely
compliments you've given me
during our friendship. You make
me feel good about myself.

*Our friendship is more
than spending time together.
Our hearts match. You have
touched my life deeply.*

If, instead of a gem
or even a flower,
we would cast the
gift of a lovely
thought into the
heart of a friend,
that would be giving
as angels give.

GEORGE
MACDONALD

The best mirror
is an old friend.

GEORGE
HERBERT

Thank you for respecting
my opinion enough to ask
for it often. You and I are
down-to-earth, practical,
helpful to each other—
the things from which
long-standing friendships grow.

When did we become such good friends? It's difficult to pinpoint the day or situation. All I know is that one morning I awoke and noticed how important you had become to my life.

We cannot tell the precise moment when friendship is formed. As in filling a vessel drop by drop, there is at last a drop which makes it run over; so in a series of kindnesses there is at last one which makes the heart run over.

SAMUEL JOHNSON

As my friend, you are ...

A sponge when I need to
soak up sorrow.
A mop when I've made a mess.
A signpost when I'm searching.
A tear when I need to cry.
A song when I want to dance.